HOW TO SURF LIKE A CALIFORNIA GIRL

APRYL YVETTE

HOW TO SURF LIKE A CALIFORNIA GIRL

EL PORTO SHARK

CONTENTS

To all who came before me, who paddled against the tide and carved their own paths in the waves, I thank you. Your courage, your resilience, and your unwavering spirit paved the way for those of us who follow. You challenged norms, shattered stereotypes, and showed the world that the ocean is a place for everyone, regardless of gender, background, or circumstance. This book is dedicated to you, the pioneers, the trailblazers, and the wave warriors who continue to inspire and empower women like me in the surf. May your passion for the ocean continue to ripple through generations to come.

Acknowledgement

I respectfully acknowledge the ancestral and unceded territories where I have lived, worked and surfed, including the lands of the Tongva, Kizh, and Chumash Nations (now Southern California), the Piscataway and Susquehannock Nations (now Maryland), the Tocobaga and Seminole peoples (now Florida), and the Edisto, Sewee, and Cusabo peoples (now South Carolina), recognizing their enduring sovereignty and stewardship of these lands.

DISCLAIMER

This book is a mix of my own surf journey and a guide to help you catch your own waves. But hey, I don't have all the answers! This is not a substitute for professional lessons, and the world of surfing knowledge is vast and ever-evolving.

Rule #1: <u>**Never turn your back on the ocean.**</u>

Important Safety Information:

- **Swimming Ability:** <u>**You must be a competent swimmer and comfortable in the ocean before attempting to surf.**</u> Surfing involves being in deep water and navigating waves, currents, and potential wipeouts. Take this seriously and do not take surfing lessons or get on a surfboard if you don't know how to swim. Don't. Seriously. Just don't.
- **Physical Condition:** Surfing requires a certain level of fitness. Assess your abilities honestly and consult a doctor if you have any health concerns. Trust me, even if you've been a swimmer or rower, you will be working new areas of your body. It's normal to have some muscle soreness after your first try and, maybe a bruise or two. Also remember that there is not one optimal body type for surfing.
- **Ocean Conditions:** Always check surf reports, tides, and potential hazards before entering the water. Never surf alone, and be aware of your surroundings.
- **Equipment:** Use appropriate and well-maintained equipment, including a surfboard, leash, and wetsuit. The necessity of the latter two is up for debate in some circles, but I always have a leash on my board and love staying warm.

· **Lessons:** If you are a beginner, taking lessons from a quali-fied surf instructor is highly recommended. They can teach you essential skills and safety protocols. Everyone, includ-ing myself, can learn something from a good instructor. Professional surfers have coaches, why wouldn't you?

The author and publisher of this book are not respon-sible for any injuries or accidents that may occur while surfing or attempting anything from this book. Always pri-oritize safety and use your best judgment in the water. Any attempt to follow the advice in this book is done so at your own risk.

<u>**Remember: The ocean is a powerful force. Treat it with respect, and never underestimate its potential dangers.**</u>

GETTING STARTED

WHAT IS A "CALIFORNIA GIRL"?

A long with millions of others, I embody the quintessential "California girl" spirit. Yet, during my formative East Coast college years, my deeply ingrained roots were often met with an unexpected degree of disbelief. This wasn't due to the undeniable fact of my Los Angeles birthplace—surely that qualifies one as a Californian, even to the most skeptical observer—but rather my dark hair color, which defiantly rejects the pervasive, stereotypical blonde image often associated with the archetype. Even the iconic Pamela Anderson, a blonde Canadian actress who became a global sensation, famously found irony in being perpetually labeled the perfect California girl, despite her origins. What, then, truly defines a California girl, if not simply hair color or a biased, superficial opinion? It is a far more profound and multifaceted identity than outward appearance or a narrow viewpoint suggests.

I am, and have always been, a California Girl, intrinsically connected to the natural world around me. I find my deepest joy dancing in the rhythmic waves, my spirit buoyed by the ocean's embrace, and I worship the sun as it casts its golden glow upon the landscape. The crisp, salty ocean breeze doesn't merely brush my skin; it calls my name, a siren song to my very soul, while the majestic mountains stand as silent, steadfast sentinels, watching over me with an ancient wisdom. I've witnessed this magnificent shoreline undergo countless transformations over the course of my lifetime, an ever-changing tapestry of nature's artistry, yet the local flora and fauna remain always familiar comforts, anchors in a world of flux. From the graceful dolphins leaping through the surf to the tiny, industrious sand crabs burying themselves in the wet sand, from the towering, mystical giant kelp forests swaying beneath the waves to the microscopic, life-sustaining plankton, every element of this vibrant ecosystem is profoundly home to me. Wherever my journey may lead me, wherever I may roam across the globe, I am always, unequivocally, a California Girl to my very core. That undeniable essence, that intrinsic connection to this land and its spirit, is something nobody can ever diminish or take from me. It is an immutable part of who I am, a birthright and a chosen identity intertwined.

So, what is a California Girl? I, for one, am but not the only example. There is more than one way to be a "California Girl" and you don't need to be in California, a certain age, or a girl to fit the description. We are not a monolith.

This book is for anyone and everyone who wants to learn basics of surfing with a few insider tips thrown in.

MY SURFING JOURNEY & INSPIRATION

Have you ever been the odd one out, the secret stepkid, the one who was bullied, or the one who doesn't quite fit the mold? If so, this book is definitely for you. It's a celebration for those who embrace their unique journeys and who find solace in the embrace of the ocean. You belong here. There are others that share your experiences, whether they look like my story or not. By telling our stories, we show others that they are not alone and give insights into worlds some have never known. There is no universal childhood experience and there is no universal surfer.

As for me, I was born in Los Angeles, my childhood a confusing blur of freeway drives between Los Angeles and Ventura Counties. It wasn't the California dream; but a nightmare. As a mixed-race kid raised in an all-white world, I was a stranger in my own home. My very identity was a battleground, my relatives fiercely denying any part of me that didn't fit their narrow vision of who I should be. They clung to their '100% European' narrative, erasing a fundamental part of myself and forcing me into a box I never belonged in.

Years older than my siblings, I wasn't just a sister; I was the built-in babysitter, the unpaid housekeeper. My childhood wasn't carefree days and scraped knees; it was a relentless cycle of chores and responsibilities. I was taught, subtly and not-so-subtly, that I was less deserving and less worthy of the simple joys and opportunities other kids took for granted. Home was no safe space; it was a minefield of emotional abuse and neglect, a place where my spirit shrunk under the weight of their expectations.

My escape was outdoors. The sun on my face, the wind in my hair, the sand between my toes – these were my refuge. The physical world, with its tangible reality, offered a stark contrast to the chaos I endured at home. Those moments of freedom, of movement, of simply *being* were the lifelines that kept me afloat in a sea of loneliness and confusion.

My obsession with the outdoors and water started early and almost turned tragic when I was around five years old. I was with my step-family in Ojai, California, a place known for its stunning valley views and those incredible pink sunsets that paint the sky. We were camping by a creek – one of those idyllic spots with lots of trees shading the banks and the water flowing over smooth, sun-warmed rocks.

I was mesmerized. I remember wading in slowly, the cool water a welcome relief from the summer heat. The water enveloping me felt like a warm embrace. Before I knew it, I was deeper, the current tugging at my little legs. I was blissfully unaware of the danger, lost in my own world of water wonder. Apparently, I'd wandered farther from the shore than anyone realized. Suddenly, I saw my relative's face, her expression shifting from relaxed enjoyment to sheer panic. She sprinted into the creek, fully clothed, and scooped me up before I could go any further. She wasn't angry, thankfully. She just laughed and joked about how she hadn't planned on going for a swim that day!

That incident definitely left an impression, but it didn't dampen my enthusiasm for all things aquatic. Growing up near the Pacific Ocean, I spent every moment that I could steal at the beaches in Ventura and Los Angeles Counties, fearlessly charging into the waves. Boogie boards, surfboards, my own two hands – I used whatever I could to navigate the ocean's energy. All of this without any formal swimming lessons! I became a student of the sea, immersing myself in oceanography, currents, and tides. I dedicated countless hours to observing the water's patterns and rhythms. It was like deciphering a hidden language - the language of the waves.

I'm a surfer, diver, swimmer, and sailor who earned a bachelor's degree with a double major in Marine Science & Chemistry. Following graduation was a fulfilling summer working with the National Oceanic & Atmospheric Administration. I furthered my education with a master's degree in Biomedical Sciences and have since collaborated with many organizations focused on ocean conservation. During the pandemic, I added American Red Cross Certified Lifeguard and International Surfing Association Level 2 Coach & Judge to my credentials. Additionally, I have published original surfing research in peer reviewed journals and presented my work at industry conferences at Stanford University and San Diego State University's Center for Surf Research.

In this book I'll share some insider tips and ocean knowledge that I've gained from my lifetime in the water.

Also, congratulations! I'm proud of you for deciding that you're going to learn to surf. It's never too late to start. I've taught people how to surf from ages 8 to almost 80. I'm rooting for you and hope to see you out in the lineup.

THE MIND GAME

New surfers can sometimes have a feeling of not being enough, doing enough, or knowing enough about surfing and their place in the ocean. They can talk down achievements and compare themselves to Olympic gold medalists and world champions. Impostor syndrome in the water is real. What goes on in the space between your ears is critical for progressing in your surfing journey.

I've seen many surfers - me included - let the space between the ears fill up with negative banter and self-doubt. Instead of being our own worst critic, we need to train our inner dialogue to be our own advocates and best friends. There are days I don't feel as confident as I would like to but a few things have helped me progress:

* **Just go!** For a long period of time, I rarely missed a morning of dawn patrol. I went to two main spots, one for bigger and one for smaller days, and would occasionally drive 1-2 hours to catch a different break. Spending time in the water watching the ocean will help you understand how it moves and how you can best navigate it.

* **Laugh when you're scared.** Wipeouts and falls are inevitable parts of the surfing experience. When they happen, it's crucial to remember that you can swim and avoid panicking. Laughter can help manage fear and it's important to acknowledge that fear is a healthy and natural response to the power of the ocean. Panic, on the other hand, can be deadly dangerous and should be avoided at all costs.

* **Figure out what is really holding you back.** I used to get nervous and scared while surfing for no apparent reason, and I would sit away from the main break. That's normal. When it happens to me, I take a step back and assess my overall schedule and life because, for me, my surfing is better when I'm happy at home.

* **Forget perfectionism.** While it's good to take your time and focus on improving your surfing skills, avoid comparing yourself to others. Focus on your own progress and enjoy the journey. You will fall, it happens. Water is going to get in your eyes, nose, and mouth. There will also be sand everywhere. It's okay and normal. Laugh it off. Remember, the best surfers are those having the most fun so strive to be a little better today than you were yesterday.

The ocean belongs to everyone, and that includes you.

PITFALLS TO AVOID

_____

1. Vague Goals

When approaching surfing, or any new activity, it's important to have clear goals and realistic expectations. Ask yourself: Do you want to stand up on your first try? Are you looking to have occasional surf sessions or a daily activity? How does surfing fit into your current lifestyle? Understanding your goals and the time commitment required will help you achieve them. Be sure to do your research and understand the financial and logistical pieces of your surfing goals.

2. Too Much, Too Soon and Impatience

It can be tempitmg to fall into the trap of trying to progress before we are ready. We may feel that once we can stand and traverse a wave we must switch to a smaller, more advanced board. However, I've observed that transitioning from an 8-9 foot starter board to one that is 2-3 feet shorter often results in sore arms, more wipeouts, fewer waves ridden, and increased frustration.

It's important to truly master your starter board before transitioning to a new one. You might find that you enjoy longboarding or mid-length surfing more than riding a shortboard. Remember, there's usually no reward for having the smallest board in the water.

3. Lack of Cross-Training

Admittedly, I wasn't always consistent with cross-training, especially in my twenties. However, when I began to take things more seriously, my surfing improved significantly. High-intensity interval training (HIIT) was particularly effective for me, but I also incorporated running, cycling, walking, stretching, and working at a standing desk into my fitness routine.

Find activities that you enjoy and that fit your lifestyle, but always consult with your doctor before starting a new exercise program. Remember to listen to your body and rest when needed. Many of us who are now in our 40s and beyond regret not taking better care of our bodies when we were younger. Stretching, staying hydrated, and allowing injuries to heal properly are essential for long-term health and well-being.

Keep an open mind, give yourself a break, and enjoy the experience!

GROUP OR INDIVIDUAL LESSONS?

Surfing is for everyone, regardless of age or background. There are many paths to learning the sport: some people are taught by their family, some discover it on their own, some attend surf camps, and others work with private coaches. You can start surfing at any time in your life. It is never too late. I've coached people of all ages, shapes, sizes, and backgrounds. All successfully rode waves and caught the stoke.

Should someone who has never surfed before take a private (individual) lesson?

The decision between group and private surf lessons isn't based on your experience level. While some benefit from individual attention, others prefer learning with friends or partners. Ultimately, there's no universal right or wrong choice - only the best option for your personal surf journey. Choose what feels most comfortable to you!

What are the benefits of a private (individual) lesson?

Other than the obvious - having the undivided attention of the instructor or coach means that all of your questions are answered and each of your moves are analyzed. You are the center of attention. For example, I send my students home with progression plans based on their individualized goals and we have months-years long relationships. For some sessions I am in the water next to the student to coach through the entire session. For others, I will be both in the water and on land for filming progress puposes. If that doesn't appeal to you....

What are the benefits of a group lesson?

You can take a lesson with your sibling, partner, parent, friend, coworker, or with people you've never met. Each situation has its benefits. For example, if you take a lesson or coaching session with a partner or close friend, you can help each other after the lesson is over and be accountability buddies.

You can do both and throughout your surfing journey. Intermediate surfers get lessons and pros still have coaches. Tune ups on your stance and form can help you at every stage.

More importantly...

Embarking on your surfing journey is an exciting and personal adventure. It's crucial to remember that everyone's path is different. Avoid comparing yourself to other surfers, particularly if you're just starting out. The learning curve varies for everyone, and even if you have experience in other board sports like skateboarding or snowboarding, there's no guarantee that you'll instantly excel at surfing.

The ocean is a powerful and unpredictable force, and mastering the art of riding waves takes time, patience, and dedication.

Some people pick it up quickly, while others may need more time to develop their skills. Don't get discouraged if you don't see immediate results. Instead, focus on enjoying the process, embracing the challenges, and celebrating your progress, no matter how small.

Remember, surfing is more than a sport; it's a lifestyle, a connection with nature, and a source of joy and fulfillment. The most important thing is to have fun, stay safe, and cherish the experience of being in the water and riding the waves. So, relax, breathe, and let the ocean guide you on your surfing journey.

SURFING ACADEMICS

Beyond the waves and the thrill of the ride, I've always been drawn to the deeper currents of surfing – its history, its cultural impact, and its connection to the human spirit. A lifelong bookworm, I was thrilled to discover a growing community of scholars dedicated to studying surfing with academic rigor.

In 2017, I met the Institute for Women Surfers, a group of incredible women exploring the intersection of surfing, gender, and social change. Being welcomed into their circle was an honor, validating my own intellectual curiosity about the sport. My journey continued with the Center for Surf Research at San Diego State University, where I presented original research along with other surf scholars at their 2019 conference. It was exhilarating to be surrounded by academics, athletes, and passionate individuals all united by a shared love of surfing.

My academic work includes peer-reviewed publications that explore the fascinating intersection of advanced analytics, surfing, and shark behavior. This interdisciplinary approach reflects the complex nature of surfing itself, a sport that blends athleticism, environmental awareness, and cultural understanding.

Through my research, I've come to appreciate the diverse origins of surfing, with concurrent roots tracing back to Polynesia, South America, and Africa. This also challenges the Eurocentric notion that people are either 'water people' or 'land people,' a binary that ignores the rich history of aquatic traditions in South America and Africa. Historical accounts reveal that while European slavers often struggled with swimming, enslaved Africans possessed remarkable aquatic skills, diving for pearls, salvaging shipwrecks, and navigating the ocean with confidence. While Hawaii holds a special honor as the birthplace of modern surfing, it's crucial to acknowledge these diverse roots and challenge the narratives that have often excluded or marginalized those non-Hawaiian, non-European, non-Australian, or non-American contributions to the sport.

GEARING UP

PICKING YOUR BOARD

Picking your first surfboard can be confusing with all the different shapes, sizes, and surfer lingo. Don't worry, this info will help you find the board to kickstart your surfing adventure.

Types of Surfboards: A Quick Overview

- **Longboards:** These majestic beasts are 9 feet or longer, offering stability and glide. They're great for cruising, learning to catch waves, and developing your balance. I believe every good quiver should have at least one of these.
- **Shortboards:** These nimble rockets are under 7 feet, designed for high-performance surfing, aerial maneuvers, and shredding steep waves. Not ideal for beginners!
- **Funboards:** These versatile boards (typically 7-8 feet) offer a balance of stability and maneuverability. This size is great all-around for many California breaks.
- **Fish:** Shorter, wider boards with a swallowtail, known for their speed and maneuverability in smaller waves. A SoCal favorite!

- **Grovelers:** Similar to fish, but often with more volume, designed to catch even the tiniest of waves. Perfect for those mushy summer days in LA County, which is why I have a very special love for the groveler in my quiver.
- **Soft Tops - "Foamies":** Beginner-friendly boards with a soft, foam top layer, ideal for learning and minimizing the risk of injuries. The mass-produced 8 foot foamie in blue and white was the joke that became a staple in many quivers. I've had one and it is another perfect board for conditions from Santa Barbara to San Diego.
- **Guns:** I don't personally recommend trying to learn on or own a gun unless you're out to charge bigger waves. I mistakenly bought a gun once but it all ended up okay. It was really "squirrely" in my opinion and too fast for the slower sets I am usually on. It was sold to someone who took it up to Northern California and bigger waves, where it belongs.

There are other types of surfboards, but we'll stick to these for the scope of our discussion in this book. Materials and shapes may evolve but basics endure.

Volume: The Secret Sauce of Floatation

Volume is the amount of space a surfboard takes up, measured in liters. It determines how much buoyancy a board has. More volume means more float, making it easier to paddle, catch waves, and stay stable. For beginners, higher volume is key. I have also found that as I get older, more volume is my good friend.

Finding the Right Fit: It's Like Finding the Perfect Pair of Shoes

Choosing the right board depends on a few factors:

- **Your Size and Weight:** Bigger surfers tend to need more volume, while smaller in stature surfers can get away with less.
- **Your Skill Level:** Beginners can use more volume and stability, while experienced surfers can handle less volume and more maneuverability.
- **The Waves You'll Be Surfing:** Different boards are designed for different wave types. In SoCal, with our mix of beach breaks, point breaks, and mushy summer conditions, having choices in your quiver will lead to more stoke.

Side note: speaking of what to have in your quiver. I recommend keeping a good boogie board in yours. I'm not talking about those flimsy things you find in the supermarket. Go to a proper surf shop and get a quality sponge and a set of fins for your feet. You will see longtime shortboarding surfers hop on boogie boards when we are coming back from an injury or long period out of the water. It's a great tool to get re-adjusted with the water and sometimes just fun to ride and the right call based on the conditions of the day.

Sizing Charts: Your Guide to Finding the Sweet Spot

Many surf shops and websites offer sizing charts that recommend board dimensions (length, width, thickness) and volume based on your height, weight, and skill level. These charts can be a helpful starting point, but it's always best to get advice from trusted experienced surfers, coaches, or surf shop staff. The foamies are great, but not every beginner will thrive with the mass-produced version. One size does not fit all, so head over to the local surf shop and get yourself fit properly for your surf stage and surf break location.

I have found that an 8-10 foot board is the best to start learning with here in Southern California.

The local surf shop can also turn you on to local shapers in your area, where you can get a custom board built specifically for you. I've got two in my quiver, a 7'8" and a 6'3.5" from the same local shaper. These are the boards that I've had the most fun on. If you watch the locals at your break, there will be a surfboard brand that many of them will ride that isn't ridden at breaks in the next county. That brand is likely the local shaper and an internet search will confirm that for you.

L.A. Local Tip: Embrace the Groveler or Fish as Your Second Board

In Los Angeles County, with our often fickle and funky waves, a groveler or fish can be your best friend. These boards excel in smaller, mushier conditions, providing the stability and paddle power you need to catch those waves and have a blast. Plus, they're fun and forgiving, allowing you to progress quickly. Once you're comfortable with your starter board, give one of these a test ride.

If I had to narrow it down, for beginners, I'd keep an 8'+ foamie and if you have the budget for a second board, a groveler or fish. This will take care of nearly 98% of the conditions in Southern California year round. As you progress, those core boards may change or need an addition.

Try More Than One

Ultimately, the best way to find the perfect board is to try a few different options. Rent boards, ask friends if you can borrow theirs, or even consider taking a lesson that includes board rentals. Board companies and local surf shops will host demo days on the beach where you can test out many boards for an actual surf session. As you gain experience, you'll develop a better sense of what works best for you and your surfing style.

THE LEASH - YOUR
LIFELINE OR NOT?

O kay, let's talk about that little cord that attaches you to your surfboard: the leash. It's a surprisingly controversial piece of equipment in the surf world. Some surfers swear by them, and wouldn't dream of paddling out without one. Others, well, they view the leash as a restriction, a hindrance to their free-spirited wave-riding experience. So, who's right? Honestly, it's up to you!

Types of Leashes: Finding Your Perfect Tether

Before you decide whether to leash up or not, let's explore the different types of leashes available:

- **Straight Leashes:** The most common type, these are simple, straightforward, and get the job done. They come in various thicknesses (choose a thicker one for bigger waves) and lengths (generally match the length of your board).
- **Coiled Leashes:** These leashes have a coiled section that stretches out when needed, reducing drag and tangling.

These are commonly used on boogie boards and stand up paddle boards.

· **Competition Leashes:** The thinner and lighter of the straight leashes, these are designed for minimal drag during competitions. I personally like competition leashes for my shortboards.

Ankle vs. Calf Leash: While ankle leashes can work for any size, calf leashes are favored by longboarders and SUPs.

To Leash or Not to Leash?

Some surfers argue that leashes are essential for safety, preventing your board from becoming a runaway projectile and potentially injuring others. They also make it easier to retrieve your board after a wipeout, conserving energy and reducing the risk of getting separated from your ride.

On the other hand, some experienced surfers prefer the freedom of riding without a leash. They argue that it allows for greater maneuverability and reduces the risk of the leash getting tangled or causing injuries. However, this approach requires a high level of skill and awareness, and a commitment to board control and etiquette.

Your Comfort is Key

The choice of using a leash while surfing is a personal one. It's usually recommended for beginners, but with experience, you can decide what suits you best. Don't feel too pressured by outside opinions. Remember, surfing knowledge is constantly evolving, and differing viewpoints are part of the learning process.

SoCal Tip: Be Mindful of Crowds

In crowded lineups, wearing a leash becomes more than just a personal preference; it's a matter of safety and respect for those around you. Think of it this way: a runaway surfboard can be like a missile launched through the water, posing a serious risk of injury to fellow surfers. I've been on the receiving end of a runaway board and witnessed countless leashless riders lose control in wipeouts, their boards transforming into unguided projectiles. While I wholeheartedly support everyone's right to ride how they choose, in crowded breaks, ditching the leash can create a hazardous environment. Even the most skilled surfers can get caught off guard by a wave or a collision. In those moments, a leash is often the only thing preventing a potentially dangerous situation. Remember, surfing is a shared experience, and respecting the safety of others is paramount.

SHOPPING FOR WETSUITS

While the California sun might be synonymous with beaches and bikinis, a seasoned California surfer knows that a good wetsuit is essential for staying warm and comfortable in our colder Pacific Ocean waters. This section will guide you through the world of wetsuits, helping you choose the perfect armor for your surf adventures.

Wetsuit Thickness: A Balancing Act

Wetsuits are designed to trap a thin layer of water between your skin and the neoprene, which your body heat then warms up. The thickness of the neoprene determines how much insulation it provides.

For Southern California surfing, where water temperatures fluctuate throughout the year, you might need a few different wetsuit thicknesses to stay comfortable year-round.

- **Summer (July - September):** Water temperatures typically range from the mid-60s to low 70s Fahrenheit. A 2mm shorty or a spring suit (short arms and legs) is usually sufficient, but you may need more if you're hitting the water at the crack of dawn. Some warm years I've been able to "trunk it" - meaning I'm wearing board shorts and a rashguard instead of a wetsuit.

- **Fall (October - November):** As the water cools down to the high 50s and low 60s, a 3/2mm full suit (full arms and legs) becomes necessary.
- **Winter (December - March):** Water temperatures can dip into the low 50s. A 4/3mm full suit, and possibly booties and gloves, will keep you warm during those chilly winter sessions. I am a fan of booties and gloves.
- **Spring (April - June):** A 3/2mm or a spring suit will usually do the trick as the water gradually warms up.

Personal Recommendations: When it comes to wetsuits for the LA surf scene, I've got a confession: I prefer the 4/3 year round. Dawn patrol is my jam, and those early morning sessions can be chilly, even in sunny SoCal. Sure, there are those occasional summer days when I might overheat and resort to trunks and a thin 1mm jacket. Honestly, those days are rare, especially for pre-sunrise surf sessions.

Fit: Like a Glove, But Not Too Tight

A well-fitting wetsuit should feel snug but not restrictive. It should allow you to have the full range of motion while paddling and surfing. Try on different brands and sizes to find the one that fits your body shape best. Pay attention to the neck, wrists, and ankles, as these are common areas for water to seep in. If you get out of the water and have ankles that are swollen with water, there is something wrong with the fit. There are many great brands out today, some who tailor to specific demographics. Local, family owned surf shops are a great source to get fitted and buy your first wetsuit.

Features: Bells and Whistles

Wetsuits come with various features that can enhance comfort and performance. Some features to consider include:

- **Chest zip vs. back zip:** Chest zips offer better flexibility and less water entry, while back zips are easier to get in and out of.
- **Knee pads:** Provide additional durability and protection.
- **Lining:** Some suits have thermal linings for added warmth. Note that these can get quite smelly if you aren't careful.
- **Key Pocket:** If you will always need a key to your car or home, get familiar and comfortable with where the key pocket on a wetsuit is. They are usually on the arm, leg, or back and can be a pocket on the inside or outside. Be sure that you have a secure system to keep your key on land or that you are comfortable with how you'll be carrying it with you in the water.

What Do People Wear Under Their Wetsuits?

As long as I've worn a wetsuit, I've always worn a swimsuit under it. A bikini is the most convenient, being that I can maneuver keeping myself covered when changing in and out of my westuit under my changing towel. I've worn one-piece swimsuits but don't like them as much. That said, there are a good number of surfers that wear nothing. There is no right or wrong way here, only personal preference. I layer rashguards and sometimes vests in the winter.

SoCal Girl Tip: Layer Up

Layering can be a great way to stay comfortable in varying conditions. Consider wearing a rash guard or a thin neoprene vest under your wetsuit for added warmth in the winter. One winter I had a heated vest to wear under my wetsuit and those were probably the absolute best winter sessions of my entire life. Be sure that you're comfortable in layers though, some find anything more than a 4/3 too restrictive. Again, do what makes you most comfortable.

One last note, don't be afraid to try more than one gender wetsuits. While it's important to find a wetsuit that fits properly and comfortably, don't feel restricted by the gender labels on the wetsuit. It's perfectly fine to explore wetsuits designed for a different gender if you find they offer a better fit for your body type. The most important thing is to find a wetsuit that allows you to move freely and comfortably in the water. As of writing this, wetsuits are sold in sizes for kids, women, and men.

Caring for Your Wetsuit: Extending its Lifespan

Proper care is crucial for extending the life of your wetsuit and keeping it fresh. Always rinse your wetsuit thoroughly with fresh water after each use, paying special attention to the inside if it has a lining. Those cozy linings can trap sand, salt, and, let's face it, a bit of sweat, creating a breeding ground for bacteria and odors.

To ensure your wetsuit dries completely, turn it inside out and hang it in a shaded area (avoid direct sunlight, as it can degrade the neoprene). In my experience, lined wetsuits tend to develop funky smells more easily than unlined ones. If you notice a persistent odor, you can machine wash your wetsuit on the delicate cycle in cold water with a small amount of mild detergent. A splash of bleach can also help banish bacteria.

However, be warned: once a wetsuit gets truly funky it's often a lost cause. If you've tried everything and the smell lingers, it's time to retire that suit. Continuing to use a contaminated wetsuit can lead to skin irritations or infections. So, when in doubt, it's better to be safe and invest in a fresh new second skin for your surf sessions.

HAIR AND SKIN CARE
FOR SURFERS

———————————

MERMAID HAIR, DON'T CARE

Keeping hair healthy while surfing can be a challenge, especially with the combined effects of saltwater, sun, and wind. But don't worry, with a little know-how and the right hair care routine, healthy hair is possible.

Protective Styles

For those with longer hair, choosing the right hairstyle for surfing can make a big difference in minimizing tangles and breakage. Options like ponytails, braids, twists, and locs can all be effective, but the best choice depends on your individual hair type, texture, and curl pattern. There have been a number of hair covering brands of late so it is possible to find hats and other head covers that fit your needs.

I have long, textured, curly hair to my waist. In my younger days, I used to sport a ponytail, but I found that if I was being tossed around by waves it felt like my hair was being ripped out! These days, I prefer to let my hair flow freely, even if it means occasionally getting a face full of salty strands. It works for me, but it might not be the ideal solution for everyone. That said I do know many long-haired surfers of all backgrounds and genders that also leave their hair down and unbound. Experiment and find what feels most comfortable and secure for your hair type.

Pre-Surf Prep

A little pre-surf prep can go a long way in protecting your hair from the harsh effects of saltwater. Before hitting the beach, rinse your hair thoroughly with fresh water. This helps dilute the saltwater your hair absorbs, minimizing dryness and damage. You can also apply a leave-in conditioner for an extra layer of protection and moisture. I do both, my hair is wet and conditioned as I walk into the water for every session.

Post-Surf Care

After your surf session, rinse your hair again with fresh water to remove salt and sand. Follow up with a moisturizing conditioner to replenish moisture and restore your hair's pH balance. Once a week, treat your hair to a deep conditioning treatment to repair any damage and keep it healthy.

DIY Hair Care

For those with a lot of hair who surf regularly, making your own hair products can be a cost-effective and customizable option. Coconut oil and/or avocado butter are excellent base ingredients for DIY hair masks and conditioners. You can also add fragrance via essential oils and jojoba oil to adjust the consistency. Experiment with different recipes and find what works best for your hair type and needs.

Following is a base recipe with a disclaimer: this information is what I have used and works on my hair. This recipe is not recommended for anyone allergic to any of the ingredients. Before trying, assure that you don't have any sensitivities or allergies to any of the ingredients.

Apryl's Surf Hair Repair Starter:
1 cup avocado butter
0.5 cup coconut oil
1 tbsp jojoba oil
6 drops jasmine essential oil
Place all ingredients into a large bowl. Beat with a hand mixer until smooth. Place into a reusable container with a secure lid. Use as needed, which will vary depending on your hair's length and texture.

It is possible to adjust the ratio of ingredients and experiment with others like shea butter, cocoa butter, vitamin E oil, and different essential oil scents (jasmine, white hibiscus, gardenia, and sweetpea are some of my favorites).

SKIN WINS

L et's be real, surfers spend a lot of time in the sun. It's crucial to protect our skin from the harmful effects of UV exposure. Just like I rarely hit the water with dry hair, you won't often find me starting a session much past 7:00 am. Dawn patrol is my sweet spot and favorite time to surf. Not only do I relish those early morning vibes, but it's also a strategic move to avoid the sun's peak intensity. Plus, many of my favorite LA surf breaks are nestled amongst hillsides, offering a bit of natural shade during those early hours.

Even with the early starts and natural shade, I never skip the sunscreen. I will also occasionally rock a surf hat for added protection, especially on scorching summer days and at certain breaks. This is true for cloudy days as well, the sun's damaging rays still pierce through. It may not seem like one can get a sunburn or skin damage on a cloudy day but you can.

Here are a few key tips for sun protection while surfing:

Reef-Safe Sunscreens

Conventional sunscreens often contain chemicals like oxybenzone and octinoxate, which have been shown to harm coral reefs, contributing to coral bleaching and other ecological damage. To protect both your skin and the ocean, opt for reef-safe sunscreens that use mineral-based ingredients like zinc oxide or titanium dioxide. These ingredients provide effective sun protection without harming marine life.

Here are a few things to look for when choosing a reef-safe sunscreen:

- **Active Ingredients:** Check the label for "non-nano" zinc oxide or titanium dioxide.
- **Avoid Harmful Chemicals:** Steer clear of oxybenzone, octinoxate, octocrylene, and homosalate.
- **Look for "Reef-Safe" or "Coral-Safe" Labels:** Many brands now clearly label their products as reef-safe.
- **Consider Biodegradable Options:** Some sunscreens are formulated to break down more easily in the environment.

Other Sun Strategies:

Cover Up: Wear a rash guard or even a lightweight long-sleeved shirt for added protection when wetsuit free.

Seek Shade: When you're not in the water, take breaks in the shade to minimize sun exposure.

Protect Your Lips: Don't forget your lips! Use a lip balm with SPF to prevent sunburn and chapping.

Be Mindful of Reflections: Remember that water and sand reflect UV rays, increasing your exposure. I can attest to this after being on the receiving end of an uncomfortable sunburn in spite of wearing sunscreen and a hat when surfing mid-day in Fiji.

Regardless of how much melanin is in your skin, you must protect yourself. Skin burns and is damaged by the sun no matter the shade.

Outside of my surf session skin routine, I do have an entire skincare regimen. My skin responds best to mild cleansers and I use a separate day and night moisturizer. I try to keep it as simple as possible. The best thing that I ever did for my skin was to find a skin care specialist that understands my skin for facials a few times a year.

For both hair and skin, staying hydrated and moisturized is important.

UNDERSTANDING THE OCEAN

READING THE SURF FORECAST

E ver wondered how surfers always seem to know when and where the waves will be firing? It's not magic, it's all about knowing how to read a surf forecast. This section will give knowledge to help plan your surf sessions.

Swell Direction, Size, and Period: The Holy Trinity of Surf Forecasting

Think of a swell as a series of waves generated by a storm far out at sea. These swells travel across the ocean like ripples in a pond, eventually reaching our shores. To score good waves, we need to understand these three key factors:

- **Swell Direction:** This tells you where the swell is coming from (e.g., NW, SW). Surf forecasting websites use arrows or compass directions. Why does this matter? Because different surf spots work best with different swell directions. Some beaches might be perfectly angled to catch a south swell, while others might only get good waves from a west swell.

- **Swell Size:** This is the height of the waves and a bigger swell generally means bigger waves, but it's not the only factor. Pay attention to the units (feet or meters) as they can vary between regions and websites.
- **Swell Period:** This is the time between successive waves, measured in seconds. A longer period usually means a more powerful and organized swell, creating cleaner and smoother waves. Shorter periods often cause choppy or mushy conditions.

Where to Find the Info:

- **Surfline:** (www.surfline.com) This is one of the most visited surf forecast websites that offers detailed reports with swell charts, wave height graphs, and even live cams around the world. There are both free and subscription services.
- **Surf Report Apps:** There are many apps available that deliver forecasts straight to your phone. An app store search will help you find the one for your area.
- **Local Websites:** Some areas of the world have localized websites with surf cams that are either run by cities, surf shops or local surfers.

Pro Tip: Pay attention to the "rating" or "star" systems that many forecast sites use. These give you a quick indication of overall wave quality.

Wind Conditions: The Make-or-Break Factor

Wind can dramatically affect wave quality. Here's the low-down:

- **Offshore Wind:** This blows from the land out to sea, creating smoother, hollower waves. This is what every surfer dreams of!
- **Onshore Wind:** This blows from the sea towards the land, making waves choppy and messy. It can make surfing more challenging and less enjoyable.
- **Light and Variable:** This means the wind is weak or changing direction, which can be okay for surfing.

How to Interpret Wind on Forecasts:

- **Arrows:** Forecasts often use arrows to indicate wind direction.
- **Colors:** Some sites use color-coding (e.g., green for offshore, red for onshore).
- **Speed:** Wind speed is usually given in knots or can be in km/miles per hour. Stronger winds generally have a greater impact on wave quality.

Putting It All Together

To find the best surf, look for a combination of:

- **Favorable Swell Direction:** Aligned with your chosen surf spot.
- **Decent Swell Size:** Suitable for your skill level.
- **Longer Swell Period:** For cleaner, stronger waves.
- **Offshore or Light Winds:** For smooth and glassy conditions.

Extra Tips for Southern California:

- **Microclimates:** SoCal has unique microclimates, so conditions can vary between beaches even if they're close together.
- **Local Knowledge:** Talk to local surf coaches, lifeguards, or surf shop staff for real-time insights.
- **Be Patient:** Even the best forecast isn't always 100% accurate. Sometimes you just have to get out there and see for yourself!

By mastering the art of reading surf forecasts, you'll be well on your way to scoring waves.

TIDES AND CURRENTS

Surfers know that scoring waves isn't just about checking the swell forecast – you've got to understand the tides and currents too! This section will teach you how to read tide charts and navigate those sometimes-tricky currents like a seasoned pro.

Understanding Tide Charts: The Rise and Fall of the Ocean

Tides are the periodic rise and fall of sea level caused by the gravitational pull of the moon and the sun. Knowing the tides is crucial because they have a part in:

- **Wave Size and Shape:** Different surf breaks work best at different tides. Some spots might fire on a low tide, revealing sandbars that create perfect A-frames, while others might need a higher tide to have enough water over rocks or reefs.
- **Water Depth:** Low tide can expose hazards like rocks and reefs, so it's important to be aware of the depth. High tide can bring stronger currents.

Decoding the Tide Chart:

- **High Tide:** The highest point the water reaches.
- **Low Tide:** The lowest point the water reaches.
- **Incoming Tide (Flood Tide):** The period when the water level is rising.
- **Outgoing Tide (Ebb Tide):** The period when the water level is falling.

Where to Find Tide Charts:

- **Tide Chart Websites:** The National Oceanic & Atmospheric Administration (NOAA) website gives you tide charts around the United States https://tidesandcurrents.noaa.gov/
- **Surf Report Websites/Apps:** Most surf forecast sites and apps also include tide information.
- **Local News and Surf Shops:** Many will publish tide tables for the area.

How Tides Affect Surf Breaks:

- **Beach Breaks:** These often work best around mid-tide, when there's enough water but the waves aren't too mushy. Lower tides here can have closeouts, which are waves that look like a wall of water coming in and break all at once.
- **Point Breaks:** Can be good at a variety of tides, but often improve with an incoming tide.
- **Reef Breaks:** Usually require a certain amount of water to cover the reef, so they might only work well at higher tides.
- **Piers**: Surf breaks near piers are often influenced by the pilings and structures, which can create unique wave formations and currents. The pier acts as an artificial reef, causing waves to wrap and break differently than they would on a

natural shoreline, sometimes offering both lefts and rights off the same peak.

Pro Tip: Observe your local surf breaks at different tides to see how they change. This will help you predict the best conditions.

CHEMICAL OCEANOGRAPHY

E ver wonder what makes ocean water so different from the water in your shower? Chemical oceanography dives into the composition of seawater, exploring the elements and compounds that make it such a unique and dynamic environment. One of the subjects that I studied in college was marine chemistry and I've been captivated by the chemistry of our massive ocean ever since. Following is a brief iintroduction to seawater chemistry.

Salt of the Earth (or Ocean, Rather)

That salty taste? It comes from dissolved salts and minerals carried into the ocean by rivers and streams. The most abundant salt is sodium chloride (the same stuff you sprinkle on your fries!), but seawater also contains magnesium, calcium, potassium, and a whole host of other elements. This mix gives seawater its characteristic salinity, which is a measure of the dissolved salts in grams per kilogram of water. The average ocean salinity is about 35, meaning that for every kilogram of seawater, there are 35 grams of dissolved salts.

pH: The Ocean's Balancing Act

Seawater is slightly alkaline, with a pH typically between 7.5 and 8.4. This pH balance is crucial for marine life, influencing everything from the growth of coral reefs to the health of fish populations.

The pH scale measures how acidic or basic (alkaline) something is. It ranges from 0 to 14, with 7 being the neutral point. Think of it this way:

- **Lower numbers (0-6):** Things get more acidic, like lemon juice or vinegar.
- **Higher numbers (8-14):** Things get more basic, like baking soda or soapy water.
- **Right in the middle (7):** That's neutral, like pure water.

Now, here's the interesting thing: finding water that's perfectly neutral (a pH of 7) is actually pretty rare. Most water, even the stuff from your tap, has stuff dissolved in it that can shift the pH slightly one way or the other.

So, why does this matter for surfers? Well, the ocean's slightly basic (alkaline) pH can affect your skin and hair. Saltwater can dry, so it's good to be mindful of your skin and hair care after a surf session (see earlier discussion on surf hair & skin).

Other Key Measures

Chemical oceanographers also study things like dissolved oxygen, nutrients (like nitrates and phosphates), and trace elements. These factors all contribute to the complex chemical soup that is seawater and influence the health and productivity of marine ecosystems. The next time you paddle out, take a moment to appreciate the intricate chemistry beneath the surface!

SHARKS AND OCEAN SAFETY

In all of my years surfing the California coast, I've had countless encounters with marine life – dolphins leaping through the waves, sea lions popping their heads up curiously, and even the occasional stingray cruising by. When it comes to sharks, my experiences with them in the lineup have been limited.

I've only had one close encounter with a white shark while surfing. It was back in 2013, a year when my local break seemed to be a popular hangout for these magnificent creatures. I remember spotting a juvenile, maybe 4 or 5 feet long, swimming towards me. It was clearly on the hunt for smaller prey, and as soon as it noticed my presence, it quickly veered off in another direction. It was a brief but exhilarating encounter, a reminder that we share these waters with incredible creatures.

White sharks grace the entire West Coast, from California to Alaska. But here's the thing: humans are not on their menu. We're simply not part of their natural diet.

I've had the privilege of encountering white sharks up close while conducting research, and even those massive 15-footers showed no interest in taking a bite out of me. They're curious creatures, but their focus is primarily on seals, sea lions, and other marine mammals.

It's important to remember that sharks are a vital part of a healthy ocean ecosystem. They play a crucial role in maintaining balance and keeping populations of other marine animals in check. While it's natural to feel a bit apprehensive about sharing the lineup with these apex predators, understanding their behavior and respecting their presence can help us coexist peacefully.

Rest assured that local officials take shark sightings seriously. If a white shark is spotted near a surf break, they'll typically post warnings or even close the beach as a safety precaution.

The chances of encountering a shark are slim, and even if you do, it's likely to be a fleeting and awe-inspiring experience. All of that said - stay safe, listen to the local officials, and when in doubt, stay out. I don't surf in places that have had multiple shark encounters (and worse).

CATCHING WAVES

FINDING YOUR STANCE: GOOFY OR REGULAR

Figuring out your stance—whether you're "goofy" (right foot forward) or "regular" (left foot forward)—is a crucial first step in your surf journey. It determines how you'll stand on your board and affects your balance, control, and overall surfing style. How do you know which foot is your dominant one? Here are some ways to find out:

The "Push Test"

Have a friend stand behind you and unexpectedly (but gently!) give you a light push. The foot you instinctively put forward to catch yourself is likely your dominant foot. If it's your right foot, you're goofy. If it's your left, you're regular.

The "Stair Test"

Pay attention to which foot you typically use to step up first when climbing stairs. That's often your dominant foot.

Trust Your Instincts

Sometimes, you just know instinctively which foot feels more natural to put forward. Don't overthink it! If you're still unsure, try standing on a surfboard on land and see which stance feels more comfortable and balanced.

Remember, there's no right or wrong answer. Both goofy and regular stances are equally valid. The most important thing is to find what feels natural and comfortable for you. The majority of the human population will surf regular vs goofy, just like the majority of humans are right handed vs left.

PADDLING TECHNIQUES

Paddling is the foundation of surfing. It's how you get out to the waves, position yourself for takeoff, and maneuver on the wave. Mastering efficient paddling techniques will not only save you energy but also help you catch more waves and improve your overall surfing experience.

Body Positioning:

- **Lay prone on your board:** This is the position you start with on your belly and facing toward the nose (front) of your board.
- **Make a banana shape:** Your torso should be just up, bending at the waist so that your back has the shape of a banana.
- **Keep your legs together:** The most common rookie mistake I see is people allowing their legs to hug the rails of the board, leaving their feet on either side dragging in the water. When you're paddling forward, having your legs open and dragging your feet is the equivalent of having the brakes on in a car and trying to drive forward. Next time you're at the beach, watch how many people do and don't do this. By

keeping your legs together and still while you paddle, you will have an easier time. If you are on a shorter board, bending at the knees and keeping your feel out of the water is the call.

Stroke Technique:

- **Climb and Catch the water:** The paddling motion on a surfboard is like climbing a ladder rather as opposed to a stroke used when you are swimming. Reach up and then submerge your arm deep into the water, palm facing back and dig in there. You are digging in to move.
- **Pull the water towards you:** Sweep your arm back in a smooth arc, keeping your elbows close to your body.
- **Release and recover:** As your hand reaches your hip, release the water and quickly recover your arm for the next stroke. Again, this motion going back to the top should be more like climbing a ladder than a traditional swim stroke.

Paddling with one arm forward at a time is what a majority of surfers will do, but you'll see the occasional person doing both arms at the same time. I prefer one at a time.

Building Paddling Strength:
Some of the ways that I have built up my upper body strength for surfing over the years are below, use at your own risk:

- **Practice paddling drills outside of surfing:** Do prone paddleboard workouts or swim laps to improve cardiovascular endurance and upper body strength.
- **Use a resistance band or weights:** Attach a resistance band or weights to wrists and practice paddling motions on land.

· **Surf smaller waves:** Focus on paddling out and catching waves without worrying about riding them.

· **Go out and paddle when it's flat:** Sometimes it is nice to just get wet and see the ocean life when there isn't any swell. I take my biggest board out and paddle along the coast just outside of the lineup. I'll paddle 100 yards or so and then take a break by sitting on my board and admiring the scenery before going back to paddling spurts.

· **Stretching**: I stretch before, during and after surfing. Outside of surfing I have a dedicated stretching component in my everyday workouts.

RIP CURRENTS

———————————

Experienced surfers often use rip currents to their advantage. These currents, which flow away from the shore, can act like a natural "lazy river," helping you paddle out to the lineup with less effort. However, it's crucial to understand how rip currents work and how to navigate them safely, whether you're a seasoned surfer or just enjoying a day at the beach.

What is a Rip Current?

Imagine a river of water flowing out to sea, cutting through the incoming waves. That's essentially what a rip current is. They form when waves break near the shoreline, and the water that piles up needs a way to escape back out to the ocean. This escaping water often finds channels or breaks in sandbars, creating a concentrated flow that moves away from the shore.

Why Are They Dangerous?

Rip currents can be deceptively strong, sometimes moving faster than an Olympic swimmer! If you get caught in one, it can quickly pull you away from the shore. The biggest danger from one of these is panic when one is caught. Many people try to swim directly back to shore against the current, which can lead to exhaustion and even drowning.

How to Identify a Rip Current:

- **Discolored Water:** Rip currents can appear darker or murkier than the surrounding water because they are carrying sand and sediment out to sea.
- **Gaps in the Waves:** Look for areas where the waves aren't breaking as much, or where there seems to be a break in the wave pattern. This could indicate a channel where the rip current is flowing.
- **Churning Water:** The water in a rip current may appear choppy or turbulent.
- **Debris or Foam:** If you see debris or foam moving steadily seaward, it could be a sign of a rip current.

What to Do if You Get Caught in a Rip Current - Traditional Instructions:

1. **Stay Calm:** The most important thing is to not panic. Conserve your energy and remember that panic is deadly.
2. **Swim Parallel to the Shore:** Don't try to swim directly against the current. Instead, swim sideways, parallel to the shore, until you are out of the rip current.
3. **Swim Back to Shore:** Once you're out of the current, swim at an angle back to shore.
4. **If You Can't Escape:** If you're struggling or can't swim out of the current, float or tread water and wave your arms to signal for help. It's best to stay calm, which can be difficult to say the least.

What if that doesn't work?

I can personally attest to the inherent strength and unpredictable nature of rip currents, having needed assistance twice in my life. The first instance occurred when I was a young teenager, merely 13 years old, and the second about a decade ago at my familiar local surf break. In both terrifying scenarios, I found myself pulled away from the immediate shoreline, caught in a relentless circular current that seemed to mock my every effort to escape. Despite my best attempts to swim parallel to the shore, a strategy often recommended for escaping rip currents, I remained stubbornly stuck, feeling the immense power of the ocean asserting its dominance.

While some researchers propose a passive approach—to simply float and patiently wait it out, trusting that the current will eventually push you back to the shore—this can be an incredibly difficult directive to follow in the moment. Of course, this process can indeed take several minutes, and when every second away from solid ground feels like an eternity, the psychological toll can be immense. The feeling of helplessness and the vastness of the ocean around you can amplify the sense of danger, making the act of simply floating an exercise in profound mental fortitude. Understanding the dynamics of rip currents and practicing calmness, even in dire situations, can be crucial for survival.

Important Reminders:

- **Always swim or surf at a lifeguarded beach.**
- **Check with lifeguards about current conditions before entering the water.**
- **Never swim or surf alone.**
- **Learn to identify rip currents.**
- **When in doubt, don't go out!**

By understanding rip currents and knowing how to react if you get caught in one, you can significantly reduce your risk and enjoy the ocean safely.

SoCal Tip - South Swells: Strong south swells can generate stronger rip currents along Southern California beaches. Be extra cautious during these conditions.

DUCK DIVING, TURTLE ROLLS, AND THE CHICKEN WING

These are some of the essential maneuvers for getting through breaking waves and reaching the lineup.

Duck Diving:

1. **Paddle towards the wave:** Aim for a channel between waves or to a less powerful section.
2. **Push your nose down:** As the wave approaches, push the nose of your board down and dive under the wave. Going in at a slight angle helps break the water's surface tension. (If this is difficult for you because of the size of your board, move down to the Turtle Roll section.)
3. **Hold your breath:** Stay under water until the wave passes over you. We contact lens wearers do this by feel but those who don't can see when the wave passes.

4. **Surface and continue paddling:** Once you're through the wave, you angle upward, come up then continue paddling towards the lineup.
5. **Be patient:** It takes time to learn to do this. A good way to get through the waves when you're new is the Turtle Roll.

Turtle Roll:

1. **Paddle towards the wave:** Aim for a channel or a less powerful section.
2. **Keep your body flat on your board and start to turn:** As the wave approaches, stay in the prone position and begin your imitation of a turtle rolling onto its back in the water.
3. **Push down and roll:** Push down on the rail of your board and roll your body under the board as the wave passes over you.
4. **Come back around to the top and continue paddling:** Once you're through the wave, finish the roll and come back to the surface atop your board. Next, continue paddling towards the lineup. This takes practice and you won't always look smooth while doing it.

Chicken Wing:

1. **Paddle towards the wave:** Aim for a channel or a less powerful section.
2. **Dismount:** As the wave approaches, get your body on one side of your board and wrap your arm around the top of your board while holding the rail opposite to your body.
3. **Tuck underneath:** Just before the wave reaches you, tuck yourself under the wave so that it goes over your head and passes by while you and your board that you are holding are underneath.

4. **On the other side:** After the wave has passed over your head, come back up and re-orient yourself back to the paddling position.

I believe that being able to do all three is ideal.

POPPING UP

Okay, you've paddled your heart out to the lineup, found your wave and felt that surge of energy as the wave picks you up, and now it's time for the magic moment: the pop-up! The pop-up is the essential move that shifts you from lying on your board to standing and riding the wave. You've paddled hard, the wave's energy has lifted you, and now it's time for this crucial transition.

Paddle Strong: As you feel the wave lift you, give a few powerful paddles to ensure its momentum truly catches you until you feel it moving without your paddling to assist.

Hand Placement: Quickly bring your hands to the board, positioning them roughly in line with your chest. Think of creating a stable base, like a push-up position.

Push & Spring: In one fluid motion, push up with your arms while simultaneously springing your feet forward beneath you. Imagine a powerful, graceful leap, landing with your feet shoulder-width apart, knees slightly bent, and your weight centered. This is where the earlier discussion on goofy vs regular stances comes in. If you're goofy, that means that your right foot is the leading foot nearest the nose of the board and your left foot is closer to the tail of the board as you stand. For regular footers, it is the other way around. You can see this move practiced on beaches everywhere there are people learning how to surf. In fact, it is a good idea to practice this move on dry land first so that you can get the flow of it down.

Find Your Balance: Once you're on your feet, focus on your balance and stance. Keep your core engaged, your eyes looking forward, and make subtle adjustments with your feet and body to maintain stability as you ride.

Common Mistakes to Avoid:

- **Standing up too quickly:** I tell my students to wait until they felt the wave taking them, give a 1, 2 count, then pop up.
- **Paddling too late:** Start paddling early enough to be in position before the wave breaks.
- **Not looking up:** Keep your eyes focused on where you want to go, not down at your board. You will go in the direction that you are looking. Watch others when you're at your break, you can tell the wipeouts caused by looking down.
- **Rushing your stance:** Take your time to find your balance before fully standing up if you need to.

SURFING ETIQUETTE

Surfing is a shared experience, and respecting fellow surfers is essential for everyone's safety and enjoyment. Most of the world sees surfers as laid-back, however, make an etiquette mistake and you'll likely find angry surfers around you in the lineup. Here are some key etiquette guidelines to remember:

Right of Way:

- **The surfer closest to the breaking wave has priority (right of way).** This is called "dropping in" if you're the one who goes without priority and it is considered disrespectful and can be dangerous.
- **If you're unsure who has priority, err on the side of caution and give way.**
- **Communicate with other surfers:** Use eye contact, hand signals, or verbal cues to avoid misunderstandings. Don't be afraid to call your wave.

Respecting Others:

- **Don't paddle out in front of someone already riding a wave.**
- **Don't snake waves:** Don't paddle into a wave that someone else is already paddling for.
- **Don't hog the waves:** Let others have their turn.
- **Be aware of your surroundings:** Always be mindful of other surfers and avoid collisions.

General Guidelines:

- **Follow the local surf rules:** Each surf spot often has its own unwritten rules. Ask trusted local surfers or lifeguards if you're unsure.
- **Be friendly and courteous:** A positive attitude goes a long way in the surfing community.
- **Respect the ocean:** Leave no trace and be mindful of the marine environment.

By following these simple etiquette guidelines, you can help create a positive and safe surfing experience for everyone.

FINDING YOUR SURF COMMUNITY

Surfing might seem like an individual sport, but it's truly at its best when shared with others. Finding your surf community, your tribe of like-minded wave riders, can add a whole new dimension to your surfing journey.

These days, it's easier than ever to connect with fellow surfers, thanks to the power of the internet and social media. There are countless online groups and communities dedicated to celebrating diversity in surfing, offering a space for women, people of color, LGBTQ+ surfers, and other underrepresented groups to connect, share experiences, and find support.

I'm happy to see so much diversity and visibility of that diversity in the lineup these days. It's a beautiful thing to witness people from all walks of life coming together to share their love of the ocean.

If you're just starting out, the surf world might seem a bit intimidating. But trust me, there's a place for you. Start by exploring targeted hashtags and following surf shops and organizations in your area on social media. You'll quickly discover a vibrant community of fellow wave riders.

Don't be afraid to connect with other surfers online or in person. Strike up conversations in the lineup, join a local surf club, or participate in surf-related events. Before you know it, you'll have found your crew to share waves, food, and stoke with.

Even if you're not actively seeking out a surf community, simply by frequenting the same break, you'll naturally start to recognize familiar faces and build camaraderie with other regulars. Those shared experiences in the lineup, those moments of laughter and encouragement, those post-surf hangouts — they're all part of the magic that makes surfing so much more than just a sport. It's a lifestyle, a community, a connection to something bigger than ourselves.

CONCLUSION

Your Surf Journey Begins Now

As we reach the final part of this book, I hope you're feeling inspired, empowered, and ready to dive into the incredible world of surfing. Before you grab your board and paddle out, I want to leave you with a few parting thoughts.

First, let's be real: this book isn't the be-all, end-all guide to surfing. The ocean, like surfing itself, is vast and ever-evolving, full of endless nuances and discoveries. I've shared the knowledge and experiences that have shaped my own surfing journey in hopes to make this amazing sport more accessible and welcoming to everyone.

No matter your background, your identity, or your experience level, the ocean belongs to you. It belongs to us all who live on this planet. Don't let anyone tell you otherwise. There are rich and diverse aquatic and surf histories around the world, many of which have been silenced or erased in an attempt to create a narrow and exclusive narrative about who belongs in the water. I encourage you to explore and delve deeper into the fascinating work being done in surf history and equity.

Most importantly, I want you to get out there and experience the magic of surfing for yourself. Feel the rush of catching your first wave, the thrill of gliding across the water, the pure joy of being connected to something bigger than yourself. Embrace challenges, celebrate triumphs and never stop learning.

If you happen to get shacked along the way, even better! Now go catch some waves, and I'll see you in the lineup.

GLOSSARY

General Terms

Dawn Patrol refers to the practice of surfing early in the morning, typically around sunrise. It's a popular habit among surfers who want to catch the early waves before the crowds arrive and enjoy the often optimal conditions of the early morning. This is my favorite time to be in the water.

Get Barrelled / Get Shacked refers to the experience of riding inside the hollow part of a breaking wave, also known as the "barrel" or "tube." This is often considered one of the ultimate experiences in surfing, where the surfer is completely enclosed by the wave. I once got shacked on the north side of Venice Breakwater and it was amazing.

Lefts and Rights These are wave directions. If you're facing the ocean, a wave that is breaking with a surfer traveling to your right is a left. This is because the surfer has caught the wave and gone to their left. The opposite is true for rights. Most of the point breaks in Southern California are rights, and beach breaks can have both.

Snake Snaking, or to snake, is the act of paddling around, under, or over another surfer to gain the right of way on a wave. This behavior is considered poor etiquette in the surfing community as it essentially means "stealing" a wave from another surfer who had priority. Many arguments start because someone got snaked.

Stoke is a term used to express that feeling you get when you ride the waves. It embodies the joy and thrill that surfers feel when they're surfing or even just thinking about surfing. Having the stoke means being in a state of excitement or happiness related to surfing. You will know when you have the stoke.

Ocean and Wave Terms

Fetch is the unobstructed distance over which a wind blows across the water surface. It is a critical factor in determining the size and energy of the waves. The longer the fetch, the more energy is transferred to the water, generally resulting in larger waves.

Inside in surfing terminology, this refers to the area closer to the shore where waves are breaking.

Lineup is the area in the water where surfers wait to catch waves. It is typically located beyond the breaking waves, where surfers position themselves to catch the incoming swells.

Outside refers to the area further out to sea where waves are yet to break.

Period of a wave is the time it takes for two successive wave crests to pass a fixed point. It is an important parameter in wave dynamics, as it influences the wave's speed and energy. Longer periods generally indicate more powerful waves.

Swell in the ocean is a wave that carries enegry over long distances in a pattern that only starts to break and form waves when approaching shallower coastal waters. Ground swell waves tend to have longer periods and come from farther away than do wind swells which are not as strong or organized and are choppier than ground swell waves.

Tides are the rise and fall of sea levels caused by the gravitational forces exerted by the Moon and, to a lesser extent, the Sun. They are essentially very long period waves that move through the ocean, causing the sea to rise and fall along the shore. Tides have a significant impact on wave conditions, as they can alter the size and shape of the waves as they approach the shore.

Stance and Foot Positioning

Goofy stance in surfing means riding with the right foot forward and the left foot at the back of the board. This stance is less common than the regular stance and is often chosen by those who feel more comfortable leading with their right foot.

Regular stance in surfing means riding with the left foot forward and the right foot at the back of the board. This is the more common stance among surfers.

Stance refers to the position and orientation of a surfer's feet on the board. It is a fundamental aspect that affects balance, control, and the ability to perform maneuvers.

Switchfoot refers to surfing in the opposite stance to one's natural or preferred stance. For example, a regular-footed surfer would switch to a goofy stance, or vice versa. This skill enhances a surfer's versatility and ability to perform a wider range of maneuvers.

Surfboard Anatomy

Nose is the front end of the surfboard. It plays a crucial role in paddling and maneuverability. Noses can be rounded or pointed, with each shape serving different purposes. Rounded noses are common on longboards and provide stability, while pointed noses, often found on shortboards, offer better performance for turning and maneuvering.

Rails are the edges of the surfboard that run from the nose to the tail. They are crucial for determining how the board interacts with the water. Rails can be soft (more rounded) or hard (sharper), with soft rails providing stability and hard rails offering precise control and responsiveness.

Rocker refers to the curvature of a surfboard from nose to tail when viewed from the side, a critical design element that significantly influences the board's performance in various wave conditions.

Stomp Pad, also known as a **traction pad**, is located on the back end of the surfboard's deck near the tail. It provides grip and traction for the surfer's back foot, enabling powerful maneuvers without slipping. While not a structural part of the board, it is an important accessory for enhancing control and performance, especially on shortboards.

Tail is the back part of the surfboard. It significantly affects the board's speed, stability, and maneuverability. There are various tail shapes, such as squash, square, pin, round, and swallow tails, each influencing how the board performs in different wave conditions.

Surfboard Types

Fish is characterized by its unique shape, featuring a swallow tail and a relatively flat rocker. It's designed for small to medium-sized waves and offers a combination of speed and maneuverability. Fish boards are versatile and can be found in various lengths, making them suitable for different wave conditions.

Fun Shape (Funboard) is a hybrid surfboard that combines elements of longboards and shortboards. They usually range from 7 to 9 feet in length and offer a balance of stability and maneuverability. Funboards are versatile and suitable for a variety of wave conditions, making them popular among intermediate surfers.

Groveler is a type of shortboard specifically designed for small, weak waves. It typically has a wider nose and tail, more volume, and a flatter rocker compared to standard shortboards. These features provide more buoyancy and easier wave-catching capabilities, allowing surfers to perform well even in less powerful conditions.

Longboard is a classic surfboard, typically ranging from 9 to 12 feet in length. They are known for their stability and ease of paddling, making them ideal for beginners and for riding small, gentle waves. Longboards have a wide and round nose, contributing to their buoyancy and ability to catch waves easily.

Shortboard is designed for higher-performance surfing and is typically between 5'4" and 6'4" in length. They feature a pointed nose and usually a thruster fin setup, allowing for sharp turns and quick maneuvers. Shortboards are favored by experienced surfers for their responsiveness in powerful wave conditions.

About the author: Apryl is an advanced analytics expert, scientist, and surfer whose life is defined by the ocean. She is a globally recognized expert in marine science, having published in peer-reviewed journals and featured on Discovery's Shark Week, National Geographic, and PBS for her ocean conservation work. Through this book, she combines her rigorous analytical mind and decades of experience on the waves to empower women and advocate for inclusivity in the surf world.

https://www.aprylyvette.com